WE ARE FGR

A PHOTOGRAPHIC JOURNAL OF FOREST GREEN ROVERS' PROMOTION TO THE FOOTBALL LEAGUE

SHANE HEALEY & FOREST GREEN ROVERS

The History Press

Cover images: © Adam Rivers/Pro Sports Images Ltd

First published 2017

The History Press
The Mill, Brimscombe Port
Stroud, Gloucestershire, GL5 2QG
www.thehistorypress.co.uk

© Pro Sports Images Ltd with FGR, 2017

British Library Cataloguing in Publication Data.
A catalogue record for this book is available from the British Library.

ISBN 978 0 7509 8595 6

Typesetting and origination by The History Press
Printed in Turkey

If a picture is worth a thousand words, then Shane's book is a *War and Peace*-esque account of FGR's legendary promotion season. Nuff said.

Dale Vince, FGR chairman

FOREWORD

Last year was the most historic season in the history of Forest Green Rovers.

I reflect on that Wembley final almost every day – my best moment in football so far. I wake up with a smile on my face most mornings, just chuckling about it.

I think it's important that we always look back on that day with great fondness; it was such a remarkable occasion, and it shows what we can achieve even under great pressure.

We were optimistic about promotion during the season, but we were undeniably the underdogs for that Wembley final. We rose to the occasion like nobody's business, and totally dominated the game. The fans were absolutely brilliant on the day.

We celebrated long and hard. I think when you achieve something like that, you do celebrate hard. The highs are really high – they're massive – and as I said to the players, you've got to savour moments like that. You've got to enjoy it when the time's right. Then it's back down to business again – the new and exciting business of the Football League.

We'd already put in much of the hard work well before that Wembley final. You don't get into the play-offs by accident. We went into that season knowing that we could beat any team in the league on our day, and we put in some amazing performances.

The players and staff will always remember last season. I know the fans will too. Shane's book is an absolutely fantastic reminder of an unforgettable journey – and it lets us all relive those magic moments. I'll have a copy on my coffee table, and I think it's something fans of FGR through the generations will enjoy too: the season the village team got into the Football League.

Mark Cooper, FGR manager

First team squad 2016/17.

8 players handed debuts on the opening day of the season against Boreham Wood, including Sam Russell who made his second debut.

Dale Bennett, Drissa Traore and Mark Cooper in pre-season training.

Ethan Pinnock heads clear in the 1-0 opening day defeat at Boreham Wood.

The east stand in the late summer sun.

Action from the 1–1 draw with Sutton and a 1–0 victory over Gateshead.

Keanu Marsh Brown with the only goal in victory at Woking.

Matt Tubbs' stoppage time penalty in the win over York City.

A 4–1 win at Maidstone – a brace for Rhys Murphy and Christian Doidge's first for the club.

Kieffer Moore scores in a 5–1 win over Southport.

15

5-1 Forest Green's highest registered home victory was a win over Southport.

Mohamed Chemlal scores the second goal against Southport.

Darren Carter celebrates his goal in a 2–1 win at Chester.

6 The longest win sequence came in August and September after recording six straight victories.

Liam Noble and Rhys Murphy score in the match at Dover.

Rhys Murphy celebrates and Christian Doidge scores, but Dover win 4–3 in front of the TV cameras.

9,872 Facebook likes gained during the season.

Rhys Murphy celebrates his goal in the 1–1 draw with Eastleigh.

Keanu Marsh-Brown scores the only goal in a victory at home to Bromley.

148

hospitality suites purchased during the 2016–17 season.

A Sam Russell penalty save and another goal from Keanu Marsh-Brown saw victory at Braintree.

FGR ambassadors with Aarran Racine.

Two away victories at Aldershot and North Ferriby saw FGR extend their lead at the top of the table.

501

The lowest attendance for a National League involving FGR was a 3–0 away win against North Ferriby United.

Chairman Dale Vince with local school children receiving their free shirts.

Goals from Darren Carter, Christian Doidge and an own goal ensured victory at home to Guiseley.

403 shirts sold in the club shop.

A training session in the beautiful setting of Cirencester's Royal Agricultural University.

Christian Doidge in action at the 1–0 win at Solihull Moors.

1,793 The average attendance for home National League fixtures in the 2016–17 season.

Christian Doidge was the two-goal hero in victory over Aldershot.

After Aldershot thought they had snatched a draw, Christian Doidge scores in injury time.

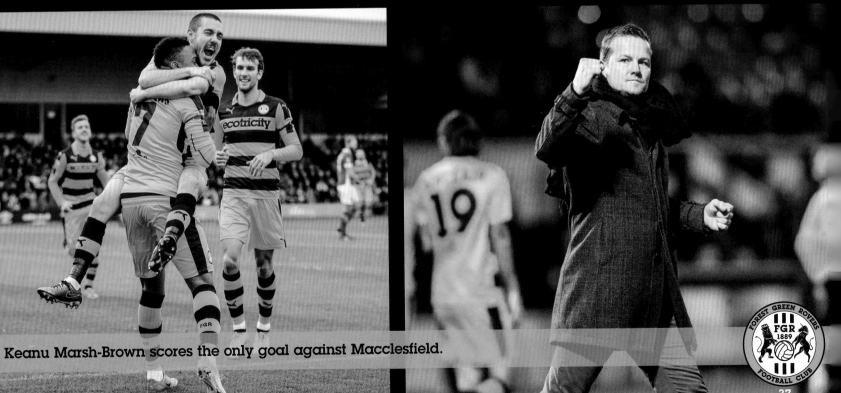

Keanu Marsh-Brown scores the only goal against Macclesfield.

545

season tickets sold for
the 2016–17 season.

Keanu Marsh-Brown scores against Lincoln City but the visitors steal the show with two late goals.

Liam Noble goes close against Tranmere.

Dale Bennett and former FGR favourite Andy Mangan.

Liam Noble scores against Tranmere Rovers.

A Darren Carter goal was the only highlight as FGR go down 3-1 at Wrexham.

42

Manny Monthe makes his first start as a Forest Green Rovers player.

43,117 fans attended National League matches at The New Lawn during the 2016–17 season.

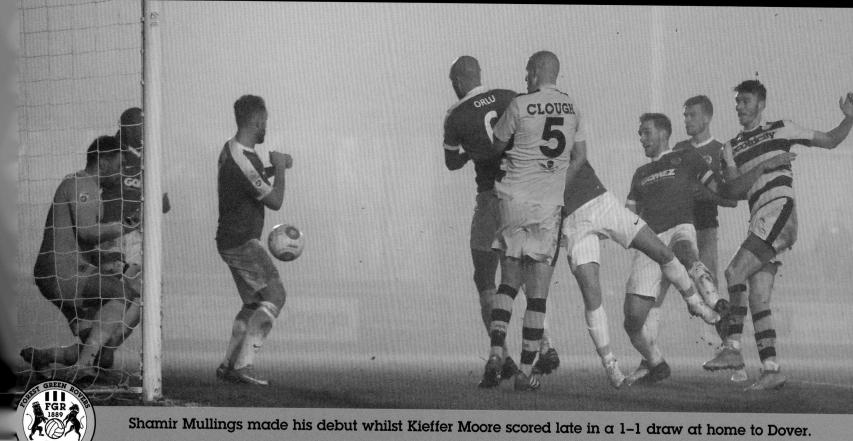

Shamir Mullings made his debut whilst Kieffer Moore scored late in a 1–1 draw at home to Dover.

Christian Doidge heads home in the 4–3 Boxing Day loss at Torquay United.

A 5–5 draw brought the New Year in with a bang with Keanu Marsh-Brown among the goal-scorers.

5-5

Forest Green's highest scoring match in the National League was a home draw with Torquay United on New Year's Day.

Elliott Frear, Keanu Marsh-Brown and Christian Doidge were on the score sheet in a 5–1 win at Bromley

Christian Doidge celebrates his goal in the 1–1 draw at Eastleigh.

5-1 The biggest away win of the season came in January 2017 with victory at Bromley.

Charlie Clough scores from a Liam Noble free kick in the 1–1 draw with Braintree.

Christian Doidge outjumps Boreham Wood's Ben Nunn.

1

Forest Green player was sent off in the 2016–17 National League season; however, Mark Ellis' red card at Sutton United was overturned on appeal.

Christian Doidge and debutant Omar Bugiel score the goals against Boreham Wood.

Sam Russell in action against his former club as FGR go down 3-1 at Gateshead.

THE EXPERTS IN GA... ...BIN...

01453 76...32

www.kerry...a...com

ONLY £50 +VAT FOR FGR SUPPORTERS

...n pest control

Omar Bugiel was the hero with two late goals to snatch a 4–3 win at home to Woking.

32 In February, Forest Green's home 4–3 win against Woking was the two clubs' thirty-second meeting at National League level. The Cards are FGR's most regularly faced opponent in the fifth tier.

Christian Doidge opened the scoring in a 3–0 win at home to Macclesfield.

58 goals conceded in the National League and play-offs during the season.

48

home goals scored by Forest Green in the National League and play-offs during the season.

Mark Ellis scores his first goal for the club, with Liam Noble also among the goals.

Christian Doidge celebrates his goal in the 2–1 defeat at Dagenham.

Dale Bennett, Liam Noble and Christian Doidge were the scorers in a 3–0 win over Wrexham.

46 away goals scored by Forest Green in the National League and play-offs during the season.

5 loan signings made during the season – Mark Ellis, Curtis Tilt, Charlie Cooper, Jake Gosling and Kaiyne Woolery.

Christian Doidge scores the winner deep into stoppage time against Solihull Moors.

Christian Doidge scores in the 3–1 defeat away to Lincoln City.

7 'doubles' with victory home and away in the division. Woking, Chester, Bromley, Aldershot, Guiseley, Solihull Moors and Macclesfield.

Charlie Cooper in action during the home defeat to North Ferriby.

94 goals scored by Forest Green in the National League and play-offs during the 2016-17 season – the most by any team in the division.

Christian Doidge heads the only goal of the match away to Guiseley.

Manager Mark Cooper watches on during the warm up at Prenton Park.

Kaiyne Woolery scores the only goal in the eighty-fifth minute at Tranmere Rovers.

6,907 The largest attendance Forest Green played in front of was at Tranmere Rovers' Prenton Park.

Liam Noble and Christian Doidge score the goals in victory over Chester.

Liam Noble strikes the second goal against Chester.

8

A 2-0 April time win over Chester was FGR's eighth win in a row in the National League since Chester reformed as a club.

Christian Doidge takes a shot during the 2–0 defeat at Southport.

4 season recruits brought in from lower levels. Ethan Pinnock transferred from Dulwich Hamlet, Manny Monthe from Bath, Omar Bugiel from Worthing and Shamir Mullings from Chelmsford City.

An own goal and a Keanu Marsh-Brown strike in the 2–2 draw with Maidstone.

19 consecutive seasons spent in the National League – a league record.

Liam Noble has a shot on goal against Maidstone.

Omar Bugiel strikes twice in a 2–2 draw which relegated York City.

A first-half Liam Noble penalty was cancelled out by Dagenham's Jordan Maguire-Drew in the first

leg play-off semi-final.

7 FGR matches were selected for television coverage on BT Sport.

The players applaud the fans who travelled to Dagenham.

Kit man Tom Carter and Liam Noble.

3,912 away supporters visited FGR during the season.

The New Lawn before the second leg play-off against Dagenham and Redbridge.

3,237 The largest attendance at The New Lawn was for the play-off semi-final second leg against Dagenham & Redbridge.

Action from the second leg and Christian Doidge scores in the thirty-fourth minute to put Rovers ahead.

4

Forest Green failed to find the net in only four National League showings against Southport, North Ferriby United, Barrow and Boreham Wood.

The south stand look on.

Keanu Marsh-Brown scores just before half-time to put FGR 2–0 ahead.

Shamir Mullings celebrates with his daughter Sienna. Sam Russell with Dad Ian.

The team celebrate reaching Wembley.

Press day at the New Lawn before the team head to London for the Promotion final.

3

North Ferriby United, Maidstone United and Solihull Moors were all opponents for the first time competitively in the history of the club during the campaign.

The players and fans arrive at Wembley Stadium.

The Forest Green Rovers Wembley dressing room.

6,982 Twitter followers gained during the season.

The prize on offer for the victors.

The players have a pre-match walkabout.

The fans excitedly await kick off.

For a second year in a row there was a sea of green at Wembley but this time they would be

5 occasions on which Forest Green clinched victory in the National League season thanks to goals in second-half stoppage time. They came in wins over Gateshead, York, Aldershot, Barrow and Solihull Moors.

going home with smiles on their faces.

Chairman Dale Vince chats to Scott Lindsay and Mark Cooper.

556

The longest journey
of the season was
to Gateshead's
International Stadium

The players warm up with Mark Cooper on the big screen.

4 players were sold during the 2016–17 season for transfer fees. Jonny Maxted switched to Guiseley, Elliott Frear to Motherwell, Charlie Clough to Barnet and Kieffer Moore to Ipswich.

Christian Doidge and Sam Russell go through their warm-up routines.

The players take a drinks break.

Christian Doidge beats Tranmere's Adam Buxton to the ball.

4 Forest Green benefitted from four own goals on their way to promotion. Kevin Lokko, Brendan Moore, Liam Daly and Jake Lawlor all put through their own net when facing FGR

Scott Lindsay and Mark Cooper give out instructions whilst Physio Ian Weston treats Drissa Traore.

Kaiyne Woolery opens the scoring in the eleventh minute.

Christian Doidge doubles Rovers lead in the forty-first minute.

27

Christian Doidge ended the season as Forest Green's top goal scorer

Christian Doidge and Kaiyne Woolery celebrate the second and third goals.

27

National League goals scored by Christian Doidge in the 2016–17 season – 8 were with his right foot, 10 with his left foot and 9 with his head.

17

clean sheets Sam Russell kept in the National League.

Kaiyne Woolery celebrates his second goal just before half-time.

The fans are in dreamland.

 Let's make history.

Our friends from Norway.

The fans celebrate Kaiyne Woolery's goal.

Full-time edges closer.

Ethan Pinnock on the ball as Mark Cooper tries to keep things calm.

Mark Ellis.

Fabien Robert was Forest Green's most used substitute in the National League.

Manager Mark Cooper shouts last minute instructions as Drissa Traore drives forward.

100% Goalkeeper Sam Russell played every minute of Forest Green's National League schedule.

As we go into added time the fans realise we are nearly there.

The final whistle goes and the players celebrate.

19 years and 170 days: Olly Mehew was the youngest National League player of the season to make an appearance.

The fans celebrate promotion to the Football League.

 **1.6**

Christian Doidge boasted a goal ratio of a successful strike every 1.6 games, while Rhys Murphy followed closely behind finding the net every 2.5 games.

Skipper Liam Noble and Dale Bennett lift the cup.

Mark Cooper shows off the trophy to the fans.

Assistant manager Scott Lindsey. Christian Doidge and Shamir Mullings.

12 Dale Bennett collected the most yellow cards in the National League for FGR.

Charlie Cooper leads the victory celebrations.

193

National League appearances Sam Russell has recorded for the club – making him the third highest ever appearance maker at that level behind Alex Meechan and Steve Perrin.

 Goalkeeping coach Steve Hale with Sam Russell.

18,801 The attendance at Wembley for the National League promotion final victory over Tranmere Rovers.

Sam Wedgebury with match-day assistant Noah Dougherty.

3

Forest Green became the third club in National League history to have lost the promotion final at Wembley one season only to return the next year to win the final. The other two clubs are Exeter City and Luton.

Celebrations with the fans.

Liam Noble shows off the cup to the jubilant supporters.

135

5 Of the selected FGR matchday squad of sixteen at Wembley for the promotion final, five players had previously appeared in finals at the stadium.

Dale Bennett, Omar Bugiel and Shamir Mullings pose in the dressing room.

Party time.

Thank you guys – 'We Are FGR, We Are Football League.'

EPILOGUE

I first started taking photography seriously only about six years ago. Some of the work I produced was not the best, but I stuck at it and in all weathers – travelling thousands of miles all across the country. Today, I am the official club photographer for Forest Green Rovers.

Most importantly though, I am a fan. I have supported the club all my life. My grandfather was captain of the team either side of World War Two, and every weekend of my childhood I would stay at my grandmother's in Lawnside at the back of the old ground. At half-time on match days, the gates would open, and you could get in for free. My friends and I would eagerly rush in and onto the pitch with our football for a kick about before the second half. We would then continue our match under the covered stand by the tea hut.

As I got older I took more notice of the matches and became a regular on the team coach travelling to away matches. The FA Vase win at Wembley in 1982 was special.

Would we ever better that?

When I left school I moved to London for nearly twenty years and I didn't get the chance see us play that often – only when we were playing somewhere local, or when I was back home visiting. Eventually, I moved back 'home' in 2003 and have been attending matches ever since.

During that time I have served on both committees of the Supporters Club and the Supporters Trust and rekindled my love of supporting at both home and away matches.

I've enjoyed taking pictures at games. There is a huge sense of pride when you capture the goal, or the emotion of a player celebrating. I really wanted to develop my skillset, so after doing my homework, I joined Pro Sports Images, a sports editorial agency. The experience I have gained since being with them has been invaluable. I have covered the Rugby World Cup, The Ashes, Premier League football, the PDC World Darts Championship and, to top it all off, the FA Cup Final.

Did I enjoy the Cup Final? Yes; however, that experience pales into insignificance when compared to the previous Sunday when my little club went to Wembley and, despite being the underdogs, beat Tranmere Rovers to reach the Football League for the first time in its history.

It is a day I will never forget. To be the photographer capturing that moment in our history was so special to me: the after-match party, being custodian of the trophy that night, the coach journey home with the team the following day. Unforgettable.

Thank you Forest Green Rovers for giving me this opportunity, I will always give this job everything. Thank you to Pro Sports Images and my fellow 'togs' for the invaluable back-up you have given me. And last, but by no means least, thank you to my wife, Virpi, and my two children, Emma and Kieran, who give me the freedom and support to do what I love.

So, what a year to make my debut. I hope you enjoy this photographic journey of the club's historic season. Hopefully the club will give me a reason to do another book in the future.

'We Are FGR, we are Football League.'

Shane Healey

2017

SUBS

Richard Atkins

Bjorn Barang & Olivier Wal's-Barang

Richard Bashford

David Booth

Anne Carter

Steve Carter

Neil Chandler – 'Happy Birthday Grampy!'

Colesy

Nigel Cooke

CR, VE, DJM & ALR Crew

Wendy Davis – 'I Love Forest Green Rovers. Well Done!'

Emma Dawkins

Bill Fletcher

Jonty Frazer

Rocco Frazer

Andrew Freeman

Ashley Fudge

Neal and Sarah Garbett

Martin Godwin

Dave Gowling

Henry Guy

Paul Haines

John Harrop – 'I am FGR!'

David Hatch

John and Pat Hatch

Emma Healey

Kieran Healey

Andrew Hodges

Charlie Hollywell

Peter Humphries

Barry Jenkins

Jokerman

Jamie Kinnear

Jahn Tore N. Kuntze

Simon Lapington

Atticus Lynham

Elian Lynham

Jan and Gerald Mauler

AndyMac

Jonathan Meaney

Viv Medcalf

Neil Munro

Harley Neate

Tom Newman

Andy Pearch – Wembley 2017

Paul Pettipher

Pitchfork and family

Poplaw Wojciech Poplawski

Les Richards

Trevor and Sharon Saunders

Jessica Smith, Uplands School Ambassador 2016/18

Lucas and Peter Smith

Steve, Sara, Grace and Maddie

Richard Stinchcomb

Jeff Taylor

Sam Taylor

The History Press

Happy 18th Birthday, Tom!

Stuart Vale

Stephen Varley

Dan Vick

Tom Vick

David Wadley

Bob and Lisa – 'What a journey!'

Clive White

Deano Whiting

John Willis

Steve Wright

'Having watched FGR for a long time, last year was the culmination of all we ever dreamt of!' – Anne and David Drew